The San Luis Valley

Gregory McNamee, SERIES EDITOR

For Linda St. Clair —
My story of a place you know well.
Blessings,

The San Luis Valley

Sand Dunes and Sandhill Cranes

Susan Tweit

TEXT BY Susan J. Tweit

San Marcos, TX

PHOTOGRAPHS BY Glenn Oakley

June 2007

The University of Arizona Press Tucson

The University of Arizona Press
Text © 2005 Susan J. Tweit
Photographs © 2005 Glenn Oakley

⊗ This book is printed on acid-free, archival-quality paper.
Manufactured in the United States of America

10 09 08 07 06 05   6 5 4 3 2 1

Library of Congress Cataloging-in-Publication Data appear on the last
printed page of this book.

Frontispiece: Great Sand Dunes and Sangre de Cristo Range

illustrations

acknowledgments

Thanks to Richard and Glenn—and Isis—for their company and inspiration, to consummate artist Sherrie York for the map, and to my parents for teaching me to love these landscapes. My appreciation as well to Carol E. Sperling of Great Sand Dunes National Park and Preserve for the thoughtful and enthusiastic review, and to Audrey Wolk and Tom Bragg of The Nature Conservancy for directions and permission to visit TNC sites. And lastly, thanks to Greg McNamee for the nudge and to the staff at the University of Arizona Press for making a magical book real.

—*Susan J. Tweit*

Thanks to Susan and Richard for their warmth, hospitality and willingness to get up at 4:30 a.m. to visit the cranes. Also, a bow to the fine staff at University of Arizona Press for supporting our project and shepherding it along. Last but not least, con mucho amor to Katherine, my fellow artist and companion.

—*Glenn Oakley*

ACKNOWLEDG-

MENTS

X

the san luis valley
SAND DUNES AND SANDHILL CRANES

The cranes called to me one windy autumn night. I lay on the couch, absorbed in a novel when a distant sound—compelling, familiar—propelled me upright to listen. There it was again, faint but unmistakable: "khrrrrr, khrrrrr," the throaty cry of sandhill cranes.

I rushed outside to search the sky. The wind hummed in the power lines; stars spangled the heavens, but I couldn't pick out the wide-winged and long-necked forms of cranes in the darkness. As my husband, Richard, came out and put his arm around me, their voices sounded again from high overhead:

"khrrrrr, khrrrrr!" We listened as the cranes called back and forth, their tremulous and wild cries a vocal tether linking the invisible flock as the birds migrated through the night, carried on the wind.

The haunting calls grew fainter until at last the cranes were gone. Although we could not see the birds, we knew where they were headed in the moonless night: over the pass to the ponds and marshes that dot the high desert of the San Luis Valley.

Twice a year, in fall and spring, flocks of sandhill cranes ride the winds high above our valley, passing by without stopping on their long migration between the northern Rockies and the southern Southwest. Headed south in the fall after nesting and raising young, the cranes follow the Arkansas River through the mountains, tracing its course in the sky like an aerial highway until the river makes an abrupt left turn for the Great Plains.

There, cranes and river part, the birds to continue south to desert wintering grounds. High above our small town, the cranes circle, ascending rising air currents on wings that can reach six and a half feet, tip to tip, their long necks and legs outstretched in flight. The huge birds spiral around and around over the valley, climbing until they are just tiny dots in the span of the heavens, until they are no longer visible, their passage revealed only by the sound of their throaty voices.

Once they have gained sufficient altitude to clear 9,010-foot-high Poncha Pass, the cranes glide south, leaving the tumultuous air of the high peaks and mountain ridges behind. Over the pass, the landscape opens into a country that is neither wholly Rockies nor wholly Southwest, but a world of its own: a wedge-shaped high valley edged by serrated peaks, spreading wider as it spills downhill into the hazy skies and dusty vistas of the desert.

This is the San Luis Valley, a remote expanse about the size of the state of Connecticut that lies forgotten between two major mountain ranges in south-central Colorado. Here, North America's tallest active sand dunes blow up against glacier-gouged mountain summits; the Rio Grande, one of the continent's great desert rivers, begins its journey from snowflake to saltwater; monotonous reaches of desert scrub hide verdant pocket wetlands. Sizzling hot in summer, frigid cold in winter, the valley is a big landscape, humbling in its openness, a wind-swept span that feels essentially wild despite an overlay of human presence. It is a place defined by the rhythmic movements of nature, a continuing dance of opposing forces, the long tension and sudden release of faulting crust, the pounding beat of water on rock, the bouncing cadence of wind and sand, the regular alternation of abundance and drought, the thrust and parry of male courting female in the ritual dances of sandhill cranes. The valley is as big as any myth, as paradoxical as everyday life, as seductive and sobering as existence itself.

I first visited the San Luis Valley on a childhood trip to the dunes—my family's summer wanderings took us to nearly every western national park and monument, plus many national wildlife refuges and state parks. Whenever I passed through the valley in the years since I admired the spectacular contrast of shrub desert and snow-splattered peaks, but I didn't stop to explore them. After Richard and I moved to his childhood

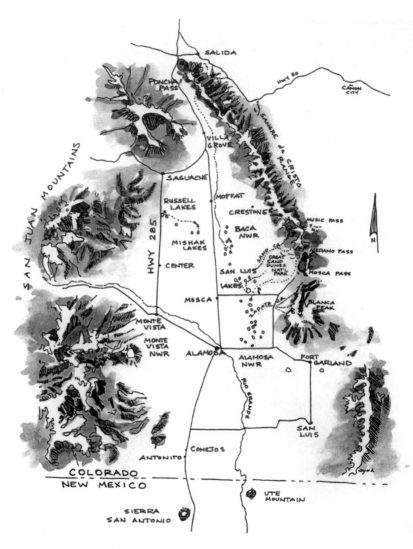

Map of the San Luis Valley (1 inch = approx. 25 miles).
Drawn by Sherrie York

hometown of Salida just over Poncha Pass from the San Luis Valley a few years ago, I learned to name and tick off the valley's landmarks like mileposts enumerating the distance home: Sierra San Antonio and Ute Mountain, the twin volcanic domes that mark its southern edge; the jutting mass of Blanca Peak, its tallest summit; the blurry brindled waves of the dunes; and the narrowing V of the upper valley pointing toward Poncha Pass and the end of our journey. Still, the San Luis Valley didn't touch my heart—until the cranes called me that windy autumn night.

Sandhill cranes arrive in the San Luis Valley twice a year some 20,000 strong to feed, rest, and socialize. The tall birds probe the soil with long beaks for insects and roots, pluck seeds from the surface, wade into the safety of shallow marshes at night, and bugle, filling the valley's air with the haunting sounds of their rich voices. After a few weeks or months, depending on the length of their journey, the cranes wing onward again, calling to each other as they follow ancient migration routes south in winter and north in spring. The San Luis Valley acts like a funnel on the Rocky Mountain flyway, guiding cranes to land in its wetlands and fields. Sandhill cranes gather there in fall on their way south, when family groups congregate in massive wintering flocks; in spring those huge flocks migrate to the valley and split up before winging north in small groups.

What makes the place attractive to cranes is the central contradiction of this high desert valley: the splotches and splashes of water that animate its arid reaches. The San Luis Valley is a desert shaped and maintained by water. Over millennia, water flushed thousands of feet of loose sediments from the surrounding mountains into this deep basin, leaving behind sheets of many-colored sand; meltwater from rivers of ice pooled in shallow lakes on the surface and permeated the pores of the layers beneath. Water and wind work in opposition: as the climate warmed and dried, the lakes vanished and eons of wind carried the sand across the valley, forming massive waves of the dunes at the foot of the mountains. Water continues to wash sand from the mountains to the valley; wind worries it loose and sets the sand in motion again.

Water is the valley's trickster: undependable, unpredictable, often hidden in plain sight. In wet seasons, water from spring snows and summer thunderstorms floods the valley floor to form isolated pools and marshes that persist for weeks or months before drying up. Streams pouring out of the mountains vanish into the ground at the edges of the valley, sucked into deep fault cracks, only to emerge elsewhere as springs—cold or hot—and shallow lakes with no outlet. These desert oases explode with life in a landscape defined by its absence, nurturing species as rare as the San Luis Valley sand hills skipper butterfly and the slender spiderflower, both found nowhere else on earth, and those as common as migrating sandhill cranes. But the valley's constant wind and relentless sun erode this veneer of verdance, ensuring aridity. As suddenly as it appeared, the water that creates the ephemeral bounty is gone, leaving only the delicate hieroglyphics of sandpiper tracks and smears of dead algae on a crust of dried clay to mark its passing.

The bulk of the valley's water hides underground, invisible

and unavailable to the arid surface in an aquifer that underlies the entire northern third of the San Luis Valley. This liquid wealth lies in a sand-and-gravel sponge thousands of feet deep with no natural outlet. A lid of clay and mineral-cemented sand caps the upper layers of this subsurface reservoir, protecting it from solar-powered evaporation; a buried underground ridge confines its downstream edge, preventing the water from reaching the valley's only out-drainage, the Rio Grande.

In flush times, the aquifer seeps upward through cracks in the layers that cap it, filling ephemeral ponds and marshes, recharging dry stream channels, and spurting out artesian wells. Like the spongy tissue in which a cactus stores water, cell by cell, the aquifer is diffused into many tiny pockets rather than concentrated; it permeates the pores in the layers beneath the surface. As with a cactus, this hidden water supply can mean the difference between life in an arid climate and death by dehydration. Without the aquifer water, the ponds, marshes, springs, and streams that water the desert would vanish and so too would the lives that depend on that fluid, including cranes.

On the first day of spring, we headed to the San Luis Valley in the darkness before dawn in search of sandhill cranes. Richard drove as the van climbed the steep grade up Poncha Pass, our friend Glenn rode shotgun with his crate of camera gear on the floor, and I sat behind with Isis, our Great Dane. Our route followed the tracks of long-vanished water paralleling the course the Rio Grande once took through what is now the high ridge of Poncha Pass.

Sandhill cranes leaving the marshes of Monte Vista Wildlife Refuge at sunrise

While water does flow uphill toward money in today's arid West, the river's ancient course through Poncha Pass is a tale of sudden force and gradual erosion, not an expensive reversal of the law of gravity. Once upon a time some thirty million years ago, as geology tells the story, after the Rocky Mountains had already heaved upward out of ancient plains, catastrophic earth movement and slow stream piracy reshaped this landscape. Back then, the Rio Grande began in the young peaks of the Rockies to the north and coursed downhill on a long southward slope, following a channel that parallels the highway we drove. Radical forces soon altered the river's drainage: continent shifting tugged the western half of North America, stretching its rock skin on an east-west axis like taffy pulled end-to-end. The crust eventually broke under the strain, splitting in long north-south faults under what is now the Southwest and Great Basin.

The strain created a rift zone, a chain of parallel fault lines spaced 50 to 100 miles apart and running from northern Mexico to Steamboat Springs, Colorado, a rent in the continental fabric so long and deep that it threatens to split the land mass in two. Like the San Andres Rift zone that ripped the peninsula of Baja California from the mainland, these fault lines could eventually create a gulf flooding the desert as far north as the San Luis Valley. (Don't rush to invest in beachfront real estate yet—geologists caution that any incursion of the ocean is millions of years away.)

The severed crust rose and fell great distances: the chunks between the fault lines dropped as much as four miles to form a series of linear, north-south-trending valleys; the edge crust, freed of the weight of the severed pieces, bobbed up in seismic spurts, forming mountain ranges. The continent tugging caused the Colorado Plateau, a Utah-sized layer cake of rock, to rotate slowly in a clockwise direction, winching the sides the Rio Grande Rift apart to form a wedge-shaped basin, the San Luis Valley.

The heaving and wrenching continued, rearranging the landscape on a scale that is hard for humans, who think of the terrain around us as static background, to comprehend. The stories that geology tells about the restless earth seem more like ancient history, folklore rather than fact, until the earth suddenly heaves, reminding us that its motion persists and its story has not ended.

The narrow chain of mountains along the eastern fault zone edging the newly created valley bowed outward in a smooth curve until it broke mid-way along its length, creating an elbow-like kink in the range. One chunk thrust westward into the valley like the prow of some humongous ship riding desert waves. Along the western fault zone, volcanic explosions triggered by the deep fractures in the crust poured out layer after layer of lava and ash, building a many-thousands-of-feet-high mountain plateau.

Erosion slowly filled the fault-created basin with layers of boulders, cobbles, gravel, sand, and clay washed from the high country on either side, raising the valley floor from below sea level to its current elevation close to a mile and a half high. By six million years ago, the landscape looked much like today's San Luis Valley: the volcanic plateau of the San Juan Mountains edging its west side; on the east, the wall of high peaks of the Sangre de Cristo Range curving from northwest to southeast except for the westward thrust of Blanca Peak. By then, the birds we call sandhill cranes existed as well—in North America, though not necessarily in the San Luis Valley—making them among the oldest still-living avian species. (Our species would not appear for another 5.5 million years.)

My hands diagrammed the movement of the earth's crust and the shape of the resultant valley as we drove south through a landscape still invisible in the predawn darkness. I paused to sip hot chocolate from my travel cup.

"What about the cranes?" asked Glenn, struggling to grasp a place he had not yet seen.

"The accidents of geology created a trap for water," I said. "Water is the key."

Sometime between six and 1.2 million years ago, a Great Plains stream ate into what is now the Upper Arkansas River Valley and "stole" the headwaters of the Rio Grande. What was left of the mighty river began in the San Juan Mountains and flowed east to the middle of the San Luis Valley, then turned abruptly south down the rift zone. Uplift around the same time amputated the upper San Luis Valley from the river drainage, transforming it into an in-draining or "closed" basin. Water that flowed in either pooled on the surface or sank into the layers of sediments under the valley floor.

For a long time, water did flow into the valley in abundance. Between 1.8 million and 12,000 years ago, a series of glacial ages brought cold climates and reduced evaporation, though not necessarily more precipitation. Inflow saturated the in-draining basin, creating the underground reservoir of fresh water and ponding in extensive shallow lakes on the surface. Mountain snow packs accumulated rather than melting, eventually forming rivers of ice that ground out deep valleys. As the region's climate fluctuated between cold and warm, the glaciers advanced and retreated. Around the time that humans reached this continent the glaciers melted, the valley-filling playa lakes vanished and the water retreated underground.

The rivers of ice left behind tons of gravel, sand, and silt pried from the mountains. Streams ferried the glacier-ground particles to the flat valley floor. The prevailing winds, blowing out of the southwest then as now, whipped across the surface and lofted the fine sand in stinging clouds, carrying it across the valley and into the elbow in the Sangre de Cristo Range. There, the rivers of air dropped their cargo where it remains today, moving endlessly up- and downhill in the steep-sided waves of dunes. Hence the valley that sand and water built, the desert that is home to migrating sandhill cranes.

We crested Poncha Pass and cruised south on U.S. Highway 285 down the San Luis Valley, tracing both the ancient watercourse and the aerial path of sandhill cranes. By the time we passed through three-block-long Villa Grove, big enough for a post office but not for a school, dawn light etched the line of the Sangre de Cristo Range, "blood of Christ" in Spanish for the color the rocky peaks take on at sunset. The high wall built

Great Sand Dunes nestle under Blanca Peak

of alternating peaks and saddles arced southward on our left. On the right, the bumpy mass of the Cochetopa Hills, part of the San Juan volcanic plateau, remained solid black against the western sky. Past Villa Grove, Highway 285 curved southwest, following the valley's widening breadth.

Once through the village of Saguache, a corruption of a Ute Indian word meaning "blue earth," for the queerly tinted ashy soils, the highway turned south, paralleling the fault zone that defines the west edge of the valley. Growing light limned the near-level, open valley floor, dotted with the occasional house and the long arms of center-pivot irrigation sprinklers. Off to the east, some thirty miles away across the valley, we could just pick out the hazy waves of the dunes, their slopes blue-shadowed with dawn.

It was light by the time we passed through Monte Vista, one of the two largest towns in the valley with a population numbering fewer than 5,000 souls. We sped through quiet streets and south on a ruler-straight farm road to the mosaic of marshes, shrub desert, and grain fields that comprise the Monte Vista National Wildlife Refuge, home to the largest flocks of sandhill cranes. We slowed at the refuge headquarters, a small complex of red-stained wood buildings, and scanned the shallow marshes, tinted pastel pink in the dawn light. No cranes. Heading south again along the edge of the refuge, we searched the marshes and fields we passed without success.

The refuge staff had reported 18,000 sandhill cranes in residence the previous week. Where were they? Could the unusual early heat of the past month have hastened them on their northward migration? I tapped my armrest nervously as I searched the surrounding landscape.

We turned west on another farm road, then north to another marsh devoid of cranes. We stopped there to scope the surrounding landscape. As soon as we rolled down the windows, we heard the distant murmur of hundreds of crane voices. We followed the sound west on a bumpy two-track that led through salt-crusted greasewood flats, past a clump of winter-bare cottonwoods to the edge of a cornfield. There, hundreds of gray-feathered bodies clumped in the stubble, probing the soil, pairing up to leap into the air and dance, jostling each other, lifting long beaks to the ever-lighter sky, and all the while, calling in those throaty voices.

We coasted to a stop by the side of the dirt road. When Richard rolled down the side window so that Glenn could shoot pictures without disturbing the birds, their sound filled the car. A solid ribbon of "khrrrrr, khrrrrr, khrrrrr!" rolled over us, a call often described as "bugling," though it lacks the brassy character of that instrument. It's a husky and seductive sound, haunting and melodic, especially when issuing from hundreds of throats. Now and then the nasal "krek!" of a young bird punctuated the flow, like an adolescent whose voice had broken.

There were tall cranes and shorter cranes, grayer cranes and dusty brown cranes. Some stood in pairs, facing one another and practicing the ballet-like moves of crane courtship; some chased each other, feigning swordplay with their long beaks; a few hopped into the air and took wing, landing on the other side of the flock; most paced through the stubble with measured tread searching for food. Their long necks dipped in a steady up-down rhythm as their spear-like beaks worked the soil for grain and insect larvae. The sheer mass of bird life was overwhelming: a crowd of noisy, moving bodies more suited to a city street than the lonesome field in a wide open landscape of desert and marsh.

A pair began courting just a few feet away. One gray bird leaped into the air on long legs, wings spread wide, then landed, legs bent in bowing motion; the other leapt up too, then bowed; the two stretched necks upward in unison and crossed beaks in a graceful silhouette as if posing. They stepped back, bowed with wings outstretched and skinny legs bent. One leapt into the air, head to the sky, calling; the other followed. As hundreds of cranes fed and stalked and hopped around them, the pair continued their dance, facing each other as if they were completely alone, as if they were the only two cranes in the world.

Like swans, geese, ravens, and some other birds, cranes mate for life and court each other anew each year. Cranes dance though, renewing their pair bonds with ballet-like wing flourishes, graceful steps, neck and beak poses, and those throaty murmurs. These evocative courtship rituals and the birds' near-human size may be the reason that cultures around the world revere cranes. Wherever these tall birds are found, from Beringia in the Asian-North American Arctic, to Africa, to the Caribbean, their images, sounds, movements, and stories appear in art, folklore, and sacred traditions. Watching the pair of sandhill cranes dance, seemingly oblivious of the crowd around them and the human observers, my heart stirred: Who could remain unmoved

Sandhill crane landing in field, San Luis Valley

by the intimacy of their gestures and their focus on each other? Who could fail to see the intensity of their connection? Perhaps the example of sandhill cranes can teach us something about fidelity and commitment, about the importance of not taking our partners for granted.

Isis thrust her huge snout out the window with her triangular ears cocked, and whined softly. Her whole body trembled with excitement.

"Shhh!" I said, and grabbed her collar. "Don't scare the cranes."

She turned to me, the sagging lids of her brown eyes giving her a baleful look. Then she lay down with a gusty sigh.

"Click! Click! Click!" Glenn's camera shutter tripped several times in rapid succession, a series of exclamation points in the purring chorus of sandhill cranes.

I counted a nearby patch of feeding birds and extrapolated their density to the whole flock, guessing that there were at least 800 cranes, perhaps a thousand. According to the pictures in my field guide, the gray birds were adults; the brownish ones last year's young, still carrying their juvenile plumage. The taller birds are considered a separate subspecies, greater sandhill cranes. They outnumbered the shorter ones, Canadian sandhills and lesser sandhills, by about eight to two, a typical ratio for the Rocky Mountain population, biologists say. Greater sandhills are aptly named: at four feet tall and ten pounds, they have five inches on the Canadian and lesser subspecies and weigh thirty percent more. Body size and length of migration route are inversely related: greater sandhills fly the shortest routes to nesting habitat in the Northern Rockies; the smaller Canadian and lesser sandhills fly on to potholes and tundra in northern Canada, Alaska, and even Siberia, making yearly roundtrips of up to 14,000 miles. With lighter bodies and proportionately longer wings, Canadian and lesser sandhills achieve higher fuel efficiency, as it were, eking more flight miles out of each caloric consumed.

All the while we watched them, the cranes kept feeding and calling, a steady "khrrrrr, khrrrrr, khrrrrr!" issuing from hundreds of crane windpipes in a continuous wave of sound. As the sun rose over the wall of the Sangre de Cristos across the valley, the red-winged blackbirds in the nearby marsh chimed in with "churr-ee" calls, and then the meadowlarks began their melodic songs. The voices of birds filled the air, announcing the day, and the season.

"Spring," I murmured.

Glenn looked up from his camera and said, "Of course—it's spring today."

I nodded. "This is how spring should begin."

Sandhill cranes look somewhat like gray herons, but ornithologists class these ancient birds in a family all their own, distantly related to other long-legged wading birds like coots and sandpipers. They are creatures of shallow water, tied to wetlands throughout their lives: sandhill cranes winter in huge flocks in marshes and playa lakes; they break their many hundreds- or thousands-of-miles-long annual migrations at large areas of marsh or sandbar in shallow rivers; they nest in wet meadows and ponds from mountains to the Arctic. (Even the nonmigratory subspecies found in Florida, Mississippi, and Cuba reside in or near marshes.) The sandhill cranes of the Rocky Mountain flyway map their annual aerial journeys by water: river drainages guide their migration as they wing from northern Mexico and the southern Southwest to the high desert of the San Luis Valley, and then on to the northern Rockies.

Water brings the cranes to the San Luis Valley. Although snowfields splotch the region's high peaks into summer, water is in short supply in the inland west, its quantity varying radically from year to year, season to season, and month to month. The wetlands the cranes depend on are ephemeral rather than permanent habitat. Some are seasonal, fecund in winter but not summer, or crowded with competing species in one season or the other. Others flourish in wetter decades and dry up entirely in drier ones. Sandhill cranes have adapted to the inconstant nature of water in the West by staying mobile. They migrate through the year, coalescing and dispersing as they commute between wetland homes the way that bands of hunting-gathering human cultures once aggregated and split up as they moved from place to place on their seasonal rounds. Winging high above the landscape from home to home, cranes even navigate by water, following its course from place to place, using its liquid surface as a beacon, day or night.

In summer, sandhill cranes nest and raise young in small ponds, marshes, and wet meadows strewn from northern Colorado to northern Alberta. It is no simple task to find the half-dozen beaver ponds tucked in the upper reaches of a single mountain stream or the emerald dots of wet meadows punctuating seas of arid sagebrush, but the compact size and isolation of these dispersed wetlands offer near-perfect crane nesting conditions. Too small to accommodate species that nest in crowds, these mini-pantries are stocked with crane food: succulent riparian plants, plus insects, fish, frogs, and nestling birds. Their isolation means that crane nest platforms—mounds built of aquatic plants that float on the water, or perch atop beaver lodges or small islands—are safe from predators. And cranes' large and toothsome young are sheltered until they have matured enough to escape into the air.

The downside of Rocky Mountain sandhill cranes' summer refuge in the high country and far north is that winter comes early. The first frosts arrive before summer is done, signaling sandhill family groups to take wing. They journey south in slow stages, their pace and distance limited by the stamina of their young. Along the way, sandhills rest in marshes and wet meadows, joining other groups of cranes. In the inverse of their journey north, sandhill cranes aggregate into larger and larger flocks on the way south, headed for extensive wetlands that can accommodate crowds numbering in the tens of thousands. The marshes in the southern Southwest and northern Mexico provide ideal conditions, except that the timing is wrong: the low deserts are still gripped by summer's intense heat, killer conditions for cranes. Coming north in spring, sandhill cranes encounter a similar timing problem: they leave the low desert in March, before the hot weather arrives, but while ice and snow still buries their nesting habitat. Hence their lengthy twice yearly break in the San Luis Valley, allowing time for fall to cool the low desert as they wing south and spring to thaw the nesting grounds as they head north.

Sandhill crane flock in "V" formation

The valley's geographic placement where the scattered ranges of the southern Rocky Mountains coalesce into the spine of the central Rockies puts it smack in the cranes' flyway. Located at the northern edge of the Southwest and widest at the south and narrowing to the north, the valley funnels migrating birds, including sandhills. Its marshes and ponds glimmer with the promise of water, drawing cranes out of the sky.

Some 20,000 sandhill cranes congregate in the San Luis Valley each year. The flocks of long-necked, wide-winged birds are impressive, the murmur of their voices rising and falling with the rhythm of their beaks as they probe the soil in groups of hundreds or thousands, tracing lines across the blue sky as they fly from marsh and pond to field and back again, or soaring in great gyres, calling to each other, as they gather to move on their yearly rounds. Their numbers are minuscule though compared to the half-million or so sandhills that arrive on the Platte River in central Nebraska every March. What makes the much-smaller crane gathering in the San Luis Valley so memorable to me is that they make themselves at home. The hordes of sandhill cranes that visit the Platte River drop in once a year and stay for just a few weeks, like tourists. In the San Luis Valley, the cranes descend in spring and again in fall, and are in residence for as long as four months each year. Arriving in mid-February and departing by mid-April, and then winging in again on their southward journey in early September and remaining until mid-November, the sandhill cranes of the Rocky Mountain population spend as much or more time in the San Luis Valley than on either their nesting or wintering grounds. These high-desert wetlands offer more than just a resting place or sojourn; in the months the cranes pass here, loafing and feeding and dancing, they become part of the fabric of the valley, cleansing the fields of waste grain and damaging insect larvae, enriching the soil with their droppings, filling the air with their graceful dances and throaty voices.

We think of home as a single place—usually that of our birth. But in the context of cranes, sage grouse, eels, salmon, monarch butterflies, bats, whales, and all those whose lives involve a repeated cycle of moving from place to place, "home" may be better understood as the landscapes and seascapes that comprise their life's journey, rather than just one spot along the way. Perhaps for mobile lives like these, home is more complex, a pattern of places engraved in memory—either learned or genetic—and known intimately as part of a way of being that defines each species' existence. Perhaps home is any place whose call is so insistent that individuals are impelled to set out and wing or walk or swim hundreds or thousands of miles through darkness and storms, over deserts and mountain ranges, across tidal currents and rivers on journeys that mark the seasons and continue as long as their kind survive. Perhaps home is wherever we give as much as we get, the way flocks of sandhill cranes fertilize the ground where they feed and roost, any place where our voices linger in story and song and the memories of our sojourn stir hearts long after we are gone, regardless of whether we were born there or how long we stay.

The sound of a car engine blew in the van window on the morning breeze as one of the vehicles parked near us on the dirt track headed for another vantage point. A scattering of cranes nearest to the road lifted their heads as the vehicle crept by them, and birds in the edge of the flock shifted uneasily on long legs, pressing closer together. As soon as the car passed, however, the cranes resumed feeding and calling, their voices rising and falling in a rhythmic wave of sound.

During their weeks in the valley, sandhill cranes prime themselves for the remainder of their journey: they tank up on food, foraging intently for grain, starchy plant roots, succulent insect larvae, and the odd frog or snake. Biologists estimate that the big birds gain a pound or more during their stay. That may not sound impressive, but in birds weighing 7 to 10 pounds, the gain equals ten to fourteen percent of their body weight, equivalent to adding 10 to 15 pounds to a 150-pound human. Imagine launching into the air and flying 500 or so miles at altitudes up to 20,000 feet with no stops or in-flight meals—hence cranes' need to carbo-load, like marathoners before a race. When they're not eating, sandhills loaf, resting and dancing.

They also socialize, a serious endeavor for these birds. Sandhill cranes' survival on their arduous annual journeys depends on allegiances to flock, family, and pair. The months in the valley represent a transition between the relative isolation of life in small family groups and the press of months en masse with thousands of other cranes. Young birds winging south on their first migration have no experience with crowd behavior. Arriving in the valley must be like a new phase in their education, as when human children trade life at home for day care or school. Sandhill crane kids must learn everything from the sociology of groups to the science of determining what is edible to the geometry of mapping migration routes. Coming north in spring, the feeding congregations of the San Luis Valley give the brown-plumaged "teenage" cranes their final chance to hang with their cohorts in sub-adult games. For young adult cranes, those older than one year but not yet settled into pairs, springtime in the valley is perhaps analogous to a singles cruise, a chance to practice their moves and audition potential mates before the crowd disperses for the summer. For established pairs, the weeks in the valley may serve as an annual honeymoon when they renew their bonds with ritual bowing, dancing, and those throbbing calls. By the time the cranes lift off and spiral upward to continue on their way, they are fit and ready to go.

A flock of sandhill cranes against spring storm clouds, San Luis Valley

By midmorning at the Monte Vista National Wildlife Refuge the sun was warm, the wind stirring, and the flock of sandhill cranes we watched was beginning to break up. A wave of restlessness overtook the mass of birds, starting at the outer edge: first a few cranes stopped feeding, hopped a time or two, then spread their wide wings and one by one lifted off with scooping wingbeats. Then a few more birds hopped and opened their wings in flight, and a few more, until there were more cranes in the air than on the ground. The birds flew off in lines, one following another, necks outstretched, skinny legs trailing and wide wings cupping the air with powerful beats. The rush of air through wing feathers was clearly audible, rhythmic as waves lapping a distant shore. The lines of birds climbed higher and higher overhead and then flew off in all directions. Soon there were just a few hundred left in the field, feeding and calling. Richard started the van and we bumped on up the dirt track, headed off on our own journey around the valley.

Although the San Luis Valley is welcome habitat for sandhill cranes, it is a desolate and difficult place for humans. One hundred twenty miles long by more than 70 miles wide at its southern edge, the valley averages just eight inches of annual precipitation, and sits at 7,000 to 8,000 feet above sea level. The combination of aridity and high elevation makes for a harsh environment: frigid in winter, searing hot in summer, and windy and dry all year long.

Walled off from the rest of the world on two of three sides by mountain ranges whose tallest peaks reach more than 14,000 feet, isolation is a fact of valley life. Entering or leaving by road in any direction except from the south means traversing a high mountain pass. There are no Interstate highways, major airports, or shopping malls. The closest cities, Denver and Albuquerque, each lie about four hours distant. The San Luis Valley is home to around 30,000 human residents (the exact population depends on how its boundaries are drawn) in a landscape embracing nearly 5,000 square miles. That works out to about six people per square mile or three people for every two sandhill cranes. Most of the valley's human population clusters in its scattering of towns, leaving the rest of this expansive landscape very unpeopled indeed.

The human cultures of the San Luis Valley are as contradictory as the valley's nature. The south half of the valley stands firmly in the Hispanic Southwest (but with a hidden cultural twist: the original residents of the valley's oldest town, San Luis, may be descendents of Jews who converted to Catholicism before fleeing Spain in the 1600s), and the north half reflects the polyglot heritage of the Rockies. At one end of the valley, not far from the New Mexico state line rise the towers of Colorado's oldest church, a Hispanic Catholic church that watches over the impoverished sheep-ranching and railroad town of Antonito; at the other is Crestone, a village of 1,200 souls known worldwide for its concentration of spiritual centers ranging from Carmelite nuns to Tibetan Buddhists. Near the valley's center, a waving green-faced extra-terrestrial invites passersby to the metal tower of a UFO observatory overlooking a hardscrabble cattle ranch. Town names such as Alamosa ("place of the cottonwood trees") and Mosca ("fly") testify to the southern part of the valley's Hispanic heritage. In the oldest of these hamlets streets still radiate from central plazas shaded by adobe buildings and irrigation is based on historic acequias that draw from mountain streams. In the north part of the valley, newer towns with less exotic names like Center and Moffat lie amidst potato and alfalfa farms watered by modern center-pivot irrigation systems pumping groundwater.

Water weaves the story of human habitation in the San Luis Valley, beginning around 12,000 years ago with Paleo-Indians who camped around the springs and streams near the dunes to hunt the biggest of big game—giant mammoths, sloths the size of Volkswagen Beetles, and bison larger than any alive today. These Clovis people, named for the location where their fluted spear points were first identified, vanished with their giant prey around 9,000 years ago. Next came a culture that archeologists call archaic hunter-gatherers who hunted smaller game like waterfowl and rabbits, and gathered plants both from the wild and from small tended plots. These people left a rich array of rock drawings along the permanent creeks on the west side of the valley to record their comings and goings.

Sometime later, oral history tells us, the Tewa people who now live in six pueblos in northern New Mexico emerged into this world at "Sandy Place Lake," a small lake near the sand dunes. Tewa myth says this opening in the earth is also where the spirits of the dead re-enter the underworld. Taos Pueblo people mark their emergence-spot at a small lake on Blanca Peak, the massif that thrusts into the valley south of the dunes. Archeologists date both cultures' use of the valley by distinctive arrow points found around springs and lakes near the dunes, and the marshes along the Rio Grande where they hunted seasonal crowds of birds, including sandhill cranes.

Navajo oral tradition delineates their homeland by four prominent peaks marking the points of the compass. Blanca Peak, described as banded with black rock and crowned with white shell, is the mountain on the east. The "white shell" could refer to a permanent snowfield tucked in a cirque atop the peak, a lone remnant of glacial times.

Long droughts in the 1200s made life in the low deserts more tenuous and drew other Indian groups to the San Luis

Valley's dependable water. Apaches from the Southwest and Arapaho, Cheyenne, Comanches, and Kiowa from the Great Plains moved in and out of the San Luis Valley with changing seasons and political alliances. By 1400, several bands of Utes, pushed out of their home in the Great Basin by drought and other Indian groups, claimed the San Luis Valley as their summer home.

Europeans reached the valley for the first time in 1598 when a party of the Spaniard Don Juan de Oñate's expedition marched in, visited a Ute camp, and marched away. Henceforth, Spain claimed the valley and surrounding territory as its own. But the new culture left the place more or less to the Indians; for the next two centuries, Spaniards merely passed through now and then to bolster their claim, but did not stay.

Americans began eyeing the territory in the winter of 1807, when Lieutenant Zebulon Pike and a small force of men crossed either Medano or Mosca Pass in the Sangre de Cristos, struggled past the dunes, and camped on the Conejos River south of Alamosa. The point of Pike's arduous wintertime crossing of the Rockies seems to have been a spy reconnaissance of New Spain, located as it was on the western edge of the newly purchased Louisiana Territory. Not long afterward, in 1821, New Spain became Mexico, and the fledgling Mexican government—perhaps alarmed by Pike's incursion into its northern frontier—turned its attention to belatedly settling the San Luis Valley. Beginning in 1833, Mexico granted several large tracts of valley land to wealthy individuals and groups of prospective settlers.

Still, it wasn't until 1849, two-and-a-half centuries after

Oñate claimed the place for Spain that significant numbers of people of European descent actually came to stay in the San Luis Valley. These new residents were Hispanic farming and ranching families from northern New Mexico, occupying land granted by the Mexican government, yet they arrived only after America wrested the Southwest from Mexico in the Mexican-American War. (Notice the legal quagmire developing here.) These agriculturists built adobe plazas and dug acequias, communal irrigation ditches, claiming Colorado's oldest recorded water rights. As soon as the American government provided Army forts for protection against raids by the valley's earlier inhabitants, the various Indian groups, Hispanic settlements sprung up all across the southern edge of the valley, from San Luis in the east to Antonito in the west.

After our morning with the cranes, Richard, Glenn, and I sped south on Highway 285, headed for Antonito. We passed through Estrella, a handful of buildings and a junkyard next to a dry cattail marsh where in one wet spring we had spotted five long-billed curlews, rare grassland sandpipers that in flight look like small cranes with improbably long, recurved bills. Then La Jara, with its brick wool barns sitting empty next to the railroad tracks, relics of the days when herds of sheep grazed the valley and adjacent mountains; Bountiful, a siding whose name reflects the optimism of the agricultural boom in the late 1800s and early 1900s; and Romeo, marked by twin grain elevators bearing the legend "Coors" and "High-altitude Barley."

Just past the snowmelt rush of the Conejos River, we turned west to Colorado's oldest church, a twin-towered sanctuary built of dark local volcanic rock and brick in the old town of Conejos on the outskirts of Antonito. The church is dedicated to the Virgin of Guadalupe, "Our Lady" to masses of Latin Americans. This dark-skinned representation of the Virgin Mary appeared to Juan Diego, a Mexican Indian neophyte as he hurried across a hillside in Tepeyec, near Mexico City, on his way to mass in December of 1531. The apparition directed Juan Diego to ask his Bishop to build a shrine in her honor on the spot. Juan Diego reported his experience, but the Bishop doubted: he told Juan Diego to ask Our Lady for a sign to verify the truth of her appearance.

The story says that Juan Diego then began using an alternate path across the hillside in order to avoid the spot where the Virgin Mary had appeared to him. Two days later, she materialized on his new route and directed him to gather roses growing nearby as a sign of her appearance. Juan Diego followed her instructions, wrapping the out-of-season blooms in his mantle and carrying them to the Bishop. When he unwrapped the offering, the mantle was decorated with a perfect image of the dark-skinned Virgin. Convinced by the miracle of roses in December and the ghostly image, the Bishop declared Our Lady of Guadalupe real and the New World blessed. (More than four and a half centuries would pass before the Catholic Church belatedly canonized Juan Diego in 2003.)

The back-story of the miraculous appearance of the dark-skinned Virgin Mary on a Mexican hillside does not figure in the official Catholic version: the spot where Juan Diego saw his vision was the site of a temple honoring the Aztec mother-earth-goddess *Tonantzin*, "Our Mother," that had been leveled by the Spaniards. By some accounts, Juan Diego was the son of an Aztec ruler who helped Cortés defeat his own people. Was it mere coincidence that an Aztec training in the conquering culture's spiritual order had a revelation of its supreme female figure on the site that had previously honored a powerful goddess in his old religion? Perhaps Juan Diego's vision sprung as much out of the earth where he stood and the belief of generations who had inhabited it as from the newly arrived Christianity that was attempting to conquer those people, their gods, and their landscape.

In the five centuries since she appeared, Indian and Hispanic cultures of the New World have wholeheartedly embraced the Virgin of Guadalupe. Her roots are particularly deep in the Hispanic Southwest, where her image appears on the tinted windows of "lowrider" automobiles, the walls of adobe houses and aluminum-skinned house trailers alike, on sequined t-shirts, refrigerator magnets, and tattooed arms, as well as on consecrated altars. Like the church in Conejos, many Catholic churches in the region are dedicated to Our Lady, whose miraculous appearance blessed both the native people and their landscape. To me, she stands as a symbol of a people's ability to weather catastrophic change by adapting old connections and beliefs to serve in new times. I often stop to light a candle in honor of her ancestry in New World culture and place, but on this first day of spring we were on our way to visit a very different shrine.

We headed into Antonito, a railroad town that once shipped tons of sheep and wool to distant markets and now ekes out a living on the tourists who ride the steam-powered train over scenic Cumbres Pass. Our destination was not the train station, however. We aimed for the dusty side streets on the wrong side of the tracks, drawn to El Castillo, a modern shrine springing from one man's vision. There are no signs pointing the way to El Castillo, Antonito's version of the Watts Towers in Los Angeles. What draw the eye are twin aluminum-clad towers that rise like an apparition over the tidy streets of the small town, as tall as church steeples but unlike any ecclesiastical architecture I have ever seen. Their silver nose cones glint in the sun, decorated with rows of old windows framed with beer-can ends and hubcaps arranged like architectural sequins. Faced with native rock and slogan-bearing signs, the towers are as fantastical as they are fascinating. Richard and I had long admired the shrine's unique aesthetic, but we had never before succeeded in locating its creator or learning its story.

As we stopped on the side of the gravel street next to El Castillo, Glenn exclaimed and pulled out a camera. I spotted a wiry figure on the roof of the tumbledown house in front of the shrine. Richard got out of the van and the man dusted his hands on his pants and climbed down a rickety ladder to greet us.

We shook hands with Cano ("like *Chicano*"), the shrine's creator.

"Please, come in!" he said, waving us through an arching gate woven of bent steel reinforcing bar and interlaced willow

Cano at his Castillo

twigs and inscribed "Jesus, Lord of Kings," into a yard crowded with tools and piles of scavenged materials.

Cano pointed out the features of the shrine, while Isis and Lobo, his dog, sniffed and spun in excited circles in the muddy yard. From the three-sided *nicho* built of upright bathtubs sheltering plaster statues of Our Lady, Jesus, and the Holy Family, to the tallest tower with its shining aluminum skin, the whole assemblage is constructed of salvaged materials, most from the County landfill: scrap lumber, small pieces of aluminum pieced as tidily as any prize-winning quilt, glittering panes of glass in varying sizes, carved wooden screens, angular chunks of native rock, glass bottles, and bits of silver-painted chain.

Cano began the shrine thirty years ago and continues to build the rambling complex in accordance with some internal plan. "When I need something," he said, "I look and there it is."

The two tallest towers, "The King" and "The Queen," rise fifty or so feet above the back corner of the small yard, their upper stories shingled in aluminum rectangles cut from beer cans, shiny side out. Atop the King's rounded cone, a silver-painted six-armed cross aims at the sky; the Queen's tower terminates in a flat-topped widow's walk fenced with silver poles. Vertical lines of glass brick pierce the Queen's tower like tall, narrow portholes. The missile-nose-cone-shaped King's tower is decorated with two rows of wood-framed windows trimmed by beer-can ends. Below the glittering cones, each tower is faced with angular rocks. The King's tower sports balconies plus a sign saying "El Castillo" in script formed of a length of chain painted silver. The Queen's tower looks almost Moorish, with carved wooden screens shading the third-story windows and a barn-door-like opening below.

"That is where *El Negrito* lives," said Cano. "He keeps the stove fired."

Richard looked puzzled.

"El Negrito," repeated Cano, "the Slave."

I remembered that the dark-skinned one of the Three Kings is sometimes referred to as El Negrito in Spain.

"That one," Cano said, pointing to a shorter, rectangular tower, sheathed in flat-laid rock with castellated turrets, "is The Rook." "Over there," he said, indicating the small shed housing his chestnut horse, its upper story faced with large panels of weathered wood painted in stained-glass-like patterns, "is The Knight."

"The dragon goes there," Cano gestured at the flat second-story roof. "Its head over the street and its tail the other way. I haven't built it yet," he said. "Those wires are in the way," pointing to the electric wires entering from a nearby utility pole.

Hand-painted signs dotted the shrine: "La Raza and La Tierra," "Vitamin M," "La Virgen de Guadalupe," and "Jerusalem." Two ten-foot-tall arrows plunging into the ground bore the slogans, "Alcohol and Tobacco Kills" (sic) and "Mary Jane Saves."

Richard listened intently to Cano, Glenn moved about the yard shooting photos, and Isis and Lobo played. I sat by myself in the thin shade of an apricot tree, my head whirling. I felt like Alice, without the looking glass, straying in a foreign land

I hadn't known existed, whose rules stem from a bewildering blend of Spanish Catholicism, Native American culture, and like in looking-glass-land, chess.

Spiritually, I am a Quaker, part of a religious tradition that embraces simplicity in worship and life. Culturally, I come from Northern European people who practice emotional reserve and prefer order and logic over the turbulent and sometimes messy insights of heart and spirit. Neither tradition lends itself to building fantastical backyard shrines or conversing with the apparitions of saints.

Cano is no saint. In a culture that requires our heroes look the part no matter how they act, his stained and gapping teeth, wind-polished mahogany skin, and shabby clothing would not even make the first cut for the lead in the movie version of his life. Proud one moment as he describes what he has built, disarming as he recounts a drunken fall, and then sly as he tells the story of a visitor who snapped his picture and then gave him money, Cano's manner is as much Coyote, the Native American trickster, as hero. Yet he has a hero's *ganas,* the courage to follow his vision, no matter how blurred it may sometimes be. He has a hero's creativity, the ability to literally build something out of nothing, to not only see the value in what others toss away, but to consecrate the unwanted by using it to create a monument to culture and place, to faith and mystery. Cano would not call himself a hero—"It is not me building the towers, it is God"—but his creations speak for themselves.

I understand the persistent urging of visions. The radical

acts of political and social disobedience Quakers are known for come from the urgings of an inner voice that will not be denied, from being as Quakers say, "moved by the Spirit." It is clear that Cano's backyard shrine stems from the promptings of that same Holy Spirit, from the inner voice of the Divine that Quakers believe speaks within us all.

Perhaps our most profound and courageous visions come from the wild inside us, from our connection to the sacred, born in an internal territory that lies on the border between sanity and madness and rooted in the landscapes we love. Staring at the silver towers as we drove away, I wondered if I had the guts to walk that edge.

We headed back north up Highway 285 and turned east across the valley, aimed for the sand dunes. Past tiny Manassa, home to the legendary boxer Jack Dempsey, we recrossed the Conejos River a few miles upstream from the warm springs where Pike and his crew wintered in 1807. The road climbed into a string of buttes rising out of the middle of the valley, their eroding shale layers topped with a hard sill of volcanic rock coated with desert varnish. These solitary prominences are products of the rift faulting that continues to shape the valley, their table-like tops created when lava spilling out of cracks in the over-stretched crust filled depressions in what once was the valley floor. Later erosion ate away the softer layers around them, leaving the lava sills topping buttes that stand high and lonely above the surrounding desert.

We pulled over on a deserted two-track that wound up into

the buttes and got out to walk. I squatted to look at the soil: its pale chocolate-milk-colored surface was slightly shiny and cracked into rough hexagonal patterns. I picked up a pinch and it crumbled between my fingertips, dry as face powder. While Isis roamed ahead of me, sniffing the ghosts of scent in twin-hoofed sheep prints, I looked at the plants, spaced far apart and stunted by the persistent aridity. Blue grama grass dominated the slope, growing in ground-hugging, horseshoe-shaped clumps with the open end aiming uphill. Each clump in effect formed a low dam that would capture water sheeting down the slope after spring snows or summer thunderstorms. As the plant grew slowly outward over decades or perhaps centuries, the area enclosed by its "dam" would increase, enlarging its water-catchment capacity and thus, its ability to survive.

Hidden in these isolated buttes is what may be North America's oldest turquoise mine, a deposit first worked by the Folsom people. Archeologists have traced the distinctive turquoise from this mine throughout the Southwest; a Zuni tale says that Turquoise Man took stones from it to seed another mine in New Mexico. The sky-blue gem is a gift of the valley's water: groundwater forced through cracks in the aluminum-rich volcanic and shale layers leaches out copper and other minerals; when the water evaporates, it leaves them behind in a new form—ribbons and chunks of turquoise.

Beyond the buttes flowed the narrow ribbon of the Rio Grande, on its way south to Mexico and then to the Gulf. To the east rose the Culebra Range, a segment of the Sangre de Cristos, marking the far edge of the valley. Dust devils, swirls of air powered by solar energy heating the dry ground, danced across the desert scrub. Two pronghorn lay still in a dusty swale.

This southeast corner of the valley is part of the Sangre de Cristo land grant, a million acres of what is now Colorado deeded to a group of developers by the Mexican government in 1843 in an effort to settle its northern frontier. The enormous chunk of real estate stretched nearly 30 miles from the spine of the Culebra Range to the banks of the Rio Grande and nearly 40 miles from Blanca Peak to the border of what is now New Mexico. The settlers lived in the valley and shared the right to graze, gather firewood, and hunt the forests and peaks of the Culebras, the land they called simply *La Sierra*, "The Mountain." Almost as soon as the ink dried on the grant papers, however, the legal and cultural environment changed: Mexico lost the Southwest to the United States. The immense grant was split into smaller pieces. La Sierra passed through different hands, beginning a century of conflict between the grantees and private owners. In 1960, Jack Taylor, owner of the 77,000-acre Taylor Ranch, the largest single remaining chunk of La Sierra, locked the gates against the grantees' descendents. They filed suit to regain their rights but as the legal process dragged on, violence ensued, and villages shrank as whole families moved away, unable to eke out a living without access to La Sierra.

In 2004, a court case spanning 44 years and involving nearly 100 attorneys, concluded in the thousand or so descendants winning the right to return to La Sierra. Locals are ecstatic: they believe their future depends on the mountains that are their economic and spiritual home. While I share their elation, I wonder about earlier cultures' rights. The Utes, after all, called this chunk of desert home when the Spanish government appropriated it. The Tewa emerged into this world from the lake near the sand dunes; the Taos people from a lake on Blanca Peak. The Navajo consider it part of their homeland, and the Jicarilla Apache still trek to the dunes to collect sand for ceremonies. A legal right of ownership persists only for the lifetime of the paper on which it is printed and the culture that confers it; the right of residency is more organic, measured in the persistence of myth and story, in the way a culture or people becomes part of a place over time and the place an integral part of them.

Early that afternoon, we sped north to the dunes along Highway 150, cutting across the base of Blanca Peak. The valley spread out between the mountains in a dry lake of ochre and tan. Here and there, tracings of palest spring green revealed the tracks and splotches of water. I scanned the dusty patchwork of rabbitbrush and bunchgrass for the elk that winter in the valley. Soon, I spotted movement on the edge of a dry, grassy playa. Trotting out of the shrubs in single file with heads held high on long necks was a herd of elk. We counted six, and then eight, and then twelve, and then sixteen, and still they came. In the dappled light of the shrubs their brown uppers and buttery-tan bellies were perfectly camouflaged. As soon as they left the patchwork of the shrubs, their dark backs and long necks stood out like targets on the monotone grassland. They trotted out into view one after another with drillteam precision, apparently oblivious of their obviousness, perfectly at home in their patch of desert.

Past the forest of cottonwood trees along Zapata Creek in the Nature Conservancy's Medano-Zapata Ranch, the road curves northeast, revealing the dunes, rising out of the sere bunchgrass like a desert tsunami. The waves of sand sweep up as high as 750 feet from the valley floor to knife-edge crests that seem frozen in midmovement. In the background, polka-dot piñon-juniper woodlands grade into the dark green mountain forest. As we watched, a cloud shadow raced across the dunes. The flat afternoon light tinted the bare sand in skin tones ranging from ivory through palest ochre and olive to peach and pink, red-brown, chocolate, and black.

The unusually diverse range of colors in the sand is explained by its unusually varied mineral origin: most of it comes from the distant San Juan Mountains; the rest washed out of the Sangre de Cristo Range, the mountains the dunes nestle against. More than half of the grains are fragments of volcanic rock, another third are quartz, about a fifth come from varied rocks, and less than one percent are magnetite, writes Stephen Trimble in *Great Sand Dunes: The Shape of the Wind.* The latter may form a small minority, but it is a very visible one: because magnetite is so heavy, its flecks persist after water or wind moves the lighter grains, creating distinctive black streaks on the dune surfaces.

Great Sand Dunes against the Sangre de Cristo Mountains

Each type of rock erodes into sand grains as distinct as those streaks. The volcanic grains from the San Juan Mountains are small and rounded, as scratched and dinged by wind transport as survivors of multiple demolition derbies. The grains from the Sangre de Cristos, by contrast, are on average larger, lighter colored, and coarser, a consequence of their shorter journey to the dunes and their origin in granite, quartzite, sandstone, and metamorphic rocks.

It is relatively easy to trace the mineral parentage of the five billion cubic yards of sand making up the dunes, but much less simple to figure out exactly where the sand came from and when it arrived. Geologists once believed that the sand blew in after the valley glaciers receded from the San Juan Mountains, leaving tons of sediment in the floodplain of the Rio Grande exposed to southwesterly winds. In this theory, each time the river channel shifted over the past 12,000 years, laying bare new sand, the wind picked it up and carried it across the valley to the dunes. There's one hitch to that story: two sand traps lie between riverbed and dunes. The first is the *sabkha,* an Arabic word for a sheet of sand whose grains are cemented by minerals evaporated from the groundwater into a layer as immobile as paving. This mineral-cemented crust covers much of the lower valley, capping the southern edge of the underground aquifer. Sand blown in sticks, and travels no farther. Closer to the dunes is a rippling landscape of sand sparsely vegetated by shrubs and bunchgrasses that act like windbreaks, also halting sand movement.

No one argues that the sand comprising the 5-mile-wide

by 7.5-mile-long dune field blew in on the wind or that much of it comes from the San Juan Mountains. But the floodplain of the Rio Grande may not have been the main source and/or the dunes may be much older than once thought. One theory posits that the dunes formed before the sabkha and the vegetated sand sheet, perhaps in cataclysmic storms during dry periods when the water table was far below the surface and the valley's soil was bare and unstable. A new technique for dating nonorganic buried materials by measuring the amount of electrons trapped in the crystalline framework indicates that some upper sand layers were buried 20,000 years ago, before the glaciers' final retreat. Testing deeper layers of sand might or might not reveal the age of the dunes.

Wind and water work in opposition in the dunes. Without wind, the sand would have washed downstream, headed for the Gulf of Mexico. Fortunately, the San Luis Valley has wind in abundance, blowing an average of 35 miles per hour through the year, with gusts recorded at over 90 miles per hour. The fat crescent-moon outline of the dune field, with its "horns" pointing southwest and its curve nestled into the elbow of the Sangres resembles a giant wind-shaped dune. It is easy to see why the air currents deposited the sand here: a curve in the mountain wall created by Blanca Peak's westward jut forms a pocket, cupping the southwesterly winds and their load of sand like a catcher's mitt. Three low spots in the mountains—Music, Medano, and Mosca passes—further funnel the winds.

"The dunes dance," writes Stephen Trimble. Wind and sand are partners in this choreography: when moving air hits

Ponderosa pines buried up to their necks in sand, escapement area, Great Sand Dunes

a bump in its path, it speeds up on the windward side of the bump and slows down on the lee side. When the "bump" is a sand dune, the river of air bounces sand grains uphill toward the crest and drops them in the dead air space beyond, sculpting the downwind side into a gentle slope with a steep slip face on the lee side. The result: graceful mounds with curving "arms" that point either upwind or downwind.

Change the music and the dance changes as well. With a larger supply of sand, the wind builds transverse dunes, tall ripples with spines perpendicular to the air movement. Orchestrate regular flip-flops in wind direction, such as a prevailing southwesterly wind blown backwards during storm-driven winter northeasterlies, and the dune crests regularly reverse positions between gentle windward and steep lee slopes. Shifting winds from all directions form majestic pyramid-shaped star dunes with long arms flowing outward like the 75-story tall dunes on the isolated northwest edge of Great Sand Dunes. Led by the wind, the eastern edge of the dune field is gliding uphill into the Sangre de Cristos, burying anything in its path, from single trees to whole forests.

Without water, wind and sand would dance away over the horizon. Snowmelt and rain permeate the dunes, dripping into pore spaces between the grains molecule by molecule, their weight anchoring the sand. Flowing water recycles the sand. Two creeks, Sand and Medano ("sand dune" in Spanish) partially encircle the dunes, flushing sand from the dunes' uphill edge downstream into the valley, where the wind picks it up and hurls it back onto the dune field again in a continuing cycle.

We followed the entrance road into Great Sand Dunes National Park, bound for Medano Creek, and what locals call "the beach," the broad apron of creek-deposited sand along the east edge of the dunes. We parked the van and walked a short trail through a low sand ridge, aiming for the line of cottonwood trees that delineates the edge of the creek. On hot summer weekends, the beach attracts hordes of San Luis Valley residents to wade in the shallow creek and bask in the shade of the rustling trees. But on this first morning of spring, the snowmelt from the high country hadn't yet reached the creek. There was no sign of water at all: no channel, no bars, no ripples, just an expanse of sand blasted clean by the winter winds. If my feet hadn't remembered the feel of flowing water from other visits, I would not have been able to imagine a creek here. Even the cottonwoods were dead, the result of a fire in April of 2000. All that remained between the bank where we stood and the dunes was dry sand sparsely studded with pebbles, their rounded edges the only hint of flowing water.

We trudged across the loose sand toward the mountains of dunes, watching tiny figures of people climbing to the crests. A zigzagging track down one steep face showed where someone had skied or snowboarded—in slow motion, the friction of the sand a literal drag. Soon, Isis began to lag, her steps slowing and her tongue hanging out. I bent down and felt the surface of the sand: the air temperature was 80 degrees, but the sand was hot to the touch. (In summer, the sizzling surface can burn tender skin.) Richard turned back with Isis to find shade and cool footing.

Glenn and I dug into a shaded dune slip face, searching for ghosts of winter under the dry layers of windblown sand. The interior was cold and wet, a sand refrigerator. On one dune, the stems of blowout grass poked through the surface at regular intervals, and nearby the long white underground runners were exposed as the dune face moved on. A trail of pinprick-sized insect tracks crossed another face. We ran our hands over the surface ripples in the sand, feeling the topography created when the different sizes and weights of grains dance before the wind.

Before long, we craved water. A mile or so upstream, we could see the flow of Medano Creek, tracing a sinuous path along the edge of the dunes. We aimed for its mirage-like sheen. A trail over hummocky dunes overgrown with spiky rabbitbrush, prickly pear cactus, clumps of sand dropseed and blue grama, and the desiccated stems of last summer's prairie sunflowers led us past frozen water, a small snowbank lingering in the shade of a skunkbrush sumac. Isis lapped at the moisture, her tongue flapping. Finally, we came over the last rise and saw the creek, or at least where it ended in a swirl of yellow pollen and greenish bits of algae stuck to wet sand. Upstream, clear water rippled down the sheet of sand edging the dunes; downstream, the beach was wind-scoured and dry. As the snowmelt accelerated in the high country, the flow would progress down the beach, eventually reaching the valley floor. When the moisture from the mountains was exhausted, the creek would shrink again, retreating uphill.

A few yards above where the sand swallowed the tongue of the creek, the water spread in a braided channel fifteen to twenty feet wide, but only a few inches deep. Isis waded in, splashed upstream and then dipped her head to slurp a long drink. I immersed my hands. The water was silky smooth and cool, but not cold.

We meandered up Medano Creek for perhaps half a mile, passing small groups of people wading and splashing, sitting in lawn chairs by the stream, and building dams and castles in the wet sand. When we reached a quiet spot, Richard, Isis, and I stopped to laze next to the water. Glenn hiked on, aiming for the bend where the dune field pinched the creek against the lower slopes of the mountains.

Isis and I waded the creek to explore a pool dammed by the arm of a small dune. As water flowed in, the surface level rose, undermining the slope above and creating sand avalanches that slid into the pool with small spatters. The creek would eventually break through this sandy dam and continue downhill. But when the creek dried up, the wind would scour its channel and rebuild the dune.

I lay on my belly next to the creek and watched the flowing water. I could hear the continuous soft whooshing as sand grains rolled and bounced along the rippled bottom, carried up and over the water-piled mini-dunes the way they move in air before the wind. A wavelike crest a few inches tall swept down the channel, intensifying the sound. A minute later, another crest passed by, and then another, surging down the channel in a pulsing tide.

Medano Creek and Sand Creek are rare hydrological phenomena: their flow pulses rhythmically as if regulated by a

Wall of sand dune and fracture line where sand has avalanched into Medano Creek

mechanical valve. Surges form only in the unusual combination of steep gradient and swift flow, smooth creek bottoms with an abundance of loose sand, and shallow water. Water moving quickly downhill over loose sand piles up underwater ridges; as these miniature aquatic dunes accrete grain by grain, they impede the flow like so many dams. Eventually the underwater dunes fail, releasing the stored water and sand in a pulse, spawning mini-waves a few inches high and spaced less than a minute apart at low flows to waves up to a foot high on 90-second intervals when the creek is running full. The discernable surge in the current charms the child in us all, inviting participation in the creek's pulsing dance.

Laying my hand flat on the bottom, I created an instant dam: sand grains quickly piled on the upstream side as the current slowed at my obstruction. A hole appeared on the downstream side where the water, picking up speed as it slid over my hand, sucked up sand with its increased carrying power. Fine flakes of black—the heavy magnetite grains—smeared the bottom just upstream of my hand, while a ridge of tan and brown sand, the lighter stuff, developed below the hole downstream. As soon as I picked my hand up, a surge swept the channel and the sand quickly rearranged itself into undisturbed ripples. The surges carry so much sand, writes Trimble, that Medano Creek deposits two feet of fresh sediment across its thousand-foot-wide channel each year. When the water dries up in winter, the rivers of air recycle the sand to the dunes.

I turned over on my back and looked up at the bare faces of the dunes rising from the other side of the creek, their crests crisply outlined against the blue spring sky. Once over the first ridge, the dune field is a bewildering maze of bare slopes and crests, a stark expanse of sand, sky, sun, and wind that can be as forbidding as the surging creek is welcoming. Much of the dune field is designated as wilderness. Bare of plants, searing hot at mid-day, freezing at night, dry except after the occasional rain or snow, the dunes epitomize the popular definition of desert: inhospitable and lifeless.

Inhospitable, yes: it takes a resourceful life to survive in

Pulsing waves carrying sand, Medano Creek, Great Sand Dunes

this shifting sea of sand. Lifeless, no: a handful of plant and animal species call this most desert-like of environments home. Lanceleaf scurfpea, a tough relative of sweetpea, and blowout grass, the drooping-leaved grass that traces circular patterns in the sand when the wind blows, shift with the moving sand, their underground stems creeping along when buried, then sprouting new stalks. Indian ricegrass, a bunchgrass with a cloud of spring seed heads, thrives on the water beneath the dry surface. Prairie sunflower sprouts only after summer storms, briefly tinting the dune field gold and leaving its seeds to wait for the next rain.

For animals, the sea of sand belongs to the small and those active in the cooler hours of evening and night: the pocket-sized kangaroo rat, which survives by collecting seeds, plus a surprising wealth of insects, from butterflies to giant sand treader camel crickets, odd-looking creatures with special baskets on their back legs for burrowing in the sand. Seven of the dunes' insect residents are endemic, found nowhere else in the world: the Great Sand Dunes tiger beetle, a circus beetle, one robber fly, two flower beetles, one clown beetle, and a Noctuid moth.

These unique lives might have vanished long ago, without the foresight of some redoubtable San Luis Valley ladies. In the 1920s after an entrepreneur proposed to mine the sands for gold, the members of the valley's P.E.O. clubs—educational women's organizations—began lobbying for permanent protection for the San Luis Valley's beach. In 1932, President Herbert Hoover protected the dunes and the lower portion

Great Sand Dunes

of Medano Creek in Great Sand Dunes National Monument. Today it is the valley's biggest tourist asset, attracting some 300,000 visitors each year from around the world.

The national monument established by President Hoover might have protected the dunes in perpetuity if speculators hadn't discovered the bounty of water lying beneath the upper third of this seemingly arid valley, including the dunes. This underground reservoir is estimated to contain two billion acre-feet of water, enough to supply two billion households for one year—assuming it is all fresh and economically retrievable, matters of some debate but no surety.

In 1887 a well drilled at the Empire Farm northwest of Alamosa gushed an artesian fountain. News of the water bonanza spread, drawing agricultural speculators from as far away as Europe. Three thousand artesian wells were dug in the next decade, many of which exhaled enough flammable gas along with the water that they could be lit like so many torches. Gas or no, the artesian water was poured on the desert to make it bloom. Flood irrigation quickly saturated the shaley soils, turning them to gumbo. Farmers dug miles-long drainage channels and acres of irrigated soil dried white, crusted by poisonous alkali from salts left behind by the evaporating water. By the end of World War I, what remained of the artesian-well farming boom were miles of saline soil sprouting only greasewood and saltgrass. Skeletal farmhouses from those days still dot the desert, home now to pairs of mourning doves and families of pack rats.

Still, the liquid wealth underlying the upper portion of the San Luis Valley continued to inspire speculation and dreams.

Farmers learned to flush the salts down below the root zone before planting, to water shallowly from overhead with circular-pivot irrigation systems, and to ditch around their fields to drain excess water—and its load of dissolved salts—away from their crops. Today, these circular fields produce tons of potatoes and alfalfa in summer, and as a consequence of farming methods that bare fields in winter to avoid accumulating salt, tons of powder-dry windblown soil as well. Heading home one spring afternoon, I saw what I thought was a billowing cloud of forest fire smoke in the distance. Half an hour later, I drove into a roiling brown fog. The sun vanished, along with the landscape on either side of the highway. Squinting in the metallic light, I realized that the plume was not smoke, rather San Luis Valley topsoil on its way downwind. Without groundwater to wet its surface, the valley simply blows away—hence the billowing clouds of soil, and the dunes.

Some of the valley's groundwater is headed downstream fast. Beginning in 1972, the federal government's Closed Basin Project inserted a giant straw into the aquifer and began sucking out 100,000 acre-feet of water each year—enough to supply some 400,000 people. A series of wells, siphons, and canals reroute the underground supply into the Rio Grande to satisfy legal compacts with downstream states and Mexico. In the three decades since the Closed Basin Project was constructed, the upper San Luis Valley has become increasingly arid: the water table has sunk and its mosaic of seasonal ponds and marshes have shrunk. As a palliative, a share of water from the project was allocated to enlarge the Monte Vista and Alamosa

Siphon and canal, Closed Basin Project

National Wildlife Refuges and two existing wetlands in the upper valley—improvements that will last only as long as the water does.

The most audacious scheme to wring money from the valley's hidden bounty and the biggest threat to both the dunes and the valley's wetlands came out of the economic boom of the 1980s. In 1986, American Water Development filed for the right to pump 200,000 acre-feet per year of water from the aquifer under the Baca Ranch, a sprawling chunk of the valley bordering Great Sand Dunes on the north, in order to sell the water to the thirsty cities on Colorado's Front Range. The multi-million dollar scheme envisioned piping water directly through the Sangre de Cristo mountain range and down the Arkansas River, thus reversing, at a hefty cost, the geological processes that had separated the drainages millennia ago. Researchers calculated that the proposed withdrawal could lower the water table 150 feet, drying up Sand Creek and harming the dune ecosystem. Eight years after it was proposed, the project was defeated in court.

But the dream of turning water into cash didn't go away. A group of investors headed by Gary Boyce, a valley resident and former project opponent, bought the Baca Ranch and promptly proposed a similar groundwater-pumping project. An unlikely coalition of valley farmers, business people, environmentalists, and scientists led the drive to save the aquifer by purchasing the Baca Ranch and using it, plus other federal and state land, to expand Great Sand Dunes National Monument. In 2000, then-President Clinton signed an act authorizing the 150,000-acre

Great Sand Dunes National Park and Preserve adjoined by the brand new 97,000-acre Baca National Wildlife Refuge, protecting the dunes and their watershed from mountain peak to valley floor. Ironically, the expansion depended on the acquisition of the Baca Ranch from the very people who planned to mine the aquifer the future National Park would save. In 2004, after four years of legal challenges and counter-challenges, the Nature Conservancy bought the Baca Ranch and held it until September, when the federal government allocated the funds to transfer the title. The Baca, once given by the United States to the heirs of a Mexican land grant to settle their claim, finally returned to public hands. And the aquifer, plus the seasonal wetlands that dimple its surface, and the dunes, will be preserved to nourish life in abundance—including sandhill cranes.

We left the dunes late that afternoon and headed west across the Nature Conservancy's vast Medano-Zapata Ranch, a swath of valley slightly bigger than the Baca that lies immediately upwind of the dunes, encompassing both stabilized dunes and sabkha. This expansive chunk of shrub desert and sere grassland is threaded by three year-round creeks making it home to a rich array of species large and small, common and rare, including the ranch's own huge herd of bison, plus wild elk, deer, and pronghorn, some 200 species of birds, and unusual fish and endemic plants. We searched the undulating landscape for bison, but saw only their dried dinner-plate-sized "chips" littering the pavement. On a later trip, Glenn and I would head north into the portion of the ranch that will someday be included in the expanded National Park in order to visit Indian Spring, a permanent waterhole on the west edge of the dune field. In a scene straight out of San Luis Valley history, we encountered the ranch's bison herd on the move, frolicking calves and all. They flowed across the high desert hundreds strong like a furry brown river, as much at home in this arid landscape as if they had never left.

That first day of spring, the river of bison was not in view. Where the bumpy terrain of the stabilized dunes gave way to the flatter sabkha, we crossed a wide canal, brimful of water flowing between high earthen banks: the Closed Basin project, transferring water from the underground aquifer to the Rio Grande. Swallows swooped and fluttered over the manmade river, oblivious to the barbed wire fencing and signs that forbade trespassers.

Across the canal, we turned toward San Luis Lakes State Park. This small chain of shallow lakes and marshes ringed by low dunes looms large in valley history. Humans as far back as Clovis times camped on the lakeshores to hunt the enormous flocks of waterfowl drawn to this oasis. The lakes may be the site where the Tewa people emerged into this world, and they also figure in the story of how the Sangre de Cristo Range got its name: a dying Spanish priest whose party had taken shelter on a raft to escape Indians saw the sunset redden the peaks rising over the sand dunes and whispered *Sangre de Cristo,* "Blood of Christ." No matter its history and cultural significance, the main lake was dredged and the water level increased as part of the Closed Basin project, in order to improve its recreation potential. Now motorized watercraft buzz its surface, sport fisherman angle for exotic carp. Only the far lobe of the lake and several smaller lakes upstream remain more or less natural, their reaches still wild and fecund. On a birdwatching excursion to celebrate my father's 75th birthday, we spotted species after species in the untrammeled reach, from glossy ibis and yellow-headed blackbirds to white pelicans, American avocets, Forster's terns, and a pair of great horned owls on their nest.

On that first day of spring, however, the main lake had shrunk to an expanse of mud with a small puddle of water toward the far edge. The brick entrance station at the base of the hill was deserted; a hand-lettered sign on the window read "Lakes poisoned. May be hazardous to human health," referring to an unsuccessful attempt to kill the carp. We pulled into the gravel parking lot of the lakeshore picnic area with its curved metal, Jetsons-style picnic shelters to survey the scene and then headed for the road to the wildlife area. It was barred. A white dot rode on what remained of the lake: a lone white pelican, floating there just as if it still belonged.

"Let's get out of here," said Glenn.

We headed east across desert greened into farm fields and hay pastures by underground water to tiny Mosca, and then north on Colorado 17 along its ruler-straight path up the valley. A few miles north of the cluster of buildings that marks Hooper, we entered open desert again. East of the highway ran the immense swath of the Baca Ranch and future national wildlife refuge, a mosaic of desert scrub, wetland, irrigated pasture, and mountain forest stretching all the way to the high peaks of the Sangre de Cristo Range. To the west was an undulating shrubland of rabbitbrush, greasewood, and saltgrass.

"That's where Mishak Lakes is," I said to Glenn, waving my hand at the gray-green desert west of the highway.

"Where?" asked Glenn, his tone dubious as he scanned the rippled expanse, a sheet of sand and silt long ago sculpted into low dunes and now held in place by the sparse shrubs.

"Hidden in the hummocks," I said. "You can't see the ponds until you practically stumble over them. They're seasonal oases."

"Are we going there?"

"Not today," I said. "They're a summer phenomenon. We'll save them for our next trip."

Two months later, Glenn and I visited the Nature Conservancy preserve that protects these ephemeral pools. We bumped down an unmarked four-wheel-drive road, found the abandoned homestead where we were supposed to park, and set off in search of water. We crossed the overgrown homestead yard with its listing house and empty corral, threading between clumps of spiny greasewood. The soil was dry and dusty, whitened by alkali, the morning sun hot. Nothing stirred. We came to a barbed-wire fence and climbed over it. We crossed a hardpan area where the clay was still shiny and cracked into hexagonal plates that curled up at the edges, evidence of recent water. We found the channel of the seasonal creek that fills the ponds, its wide floodway almost imperceptible in the open desert, but without landmarks, we couldn't find the pools themselves. Each several-foot-high hummock and each hardpan looked just like the next. The only evidence of water was a swallow swooping through the air in the distance. As quickly as I noticed it, it vanished. I blinked, wondering if its fluttering winged-form had materialized like a mirage from my desire to show Glenn the magic wrought by water in this scrubland.

I scanned the maze of undulations, squinting in the harsh sunlight and trying to see a pond. Nothing. I cocked my ears, listening for the sound of lapping water, for birdsong, the subtle thrumming of dragonfly wings, or even the whine of mosquitoes. I heard only the dry click of mud drying and the wind. I turned my head this way and that, questing for a thread of cool, moist air. Nothing.

Glenn and I wandered for a while, heading upstream across hardpans shiny with dried clay. I knew the shallow lakes were there, somewhere, but I couldn't find them.

"You don't see them until you're right on them," I said to Glenn, raising my water bottle to chug a drink of lukewarm liquid. "You come over a bit of hummock and suddenly in front of you are pools of clear water with breeze-dappled surfaces, none bigger than an acre of two, ringed by a green fringe of sedge and rush. They're only temporary, lasting a few weeks or months, yet they burst with life: shorebirds, swallows, ducks, butterflies, gnats, dragonflies, mosquitoes, algae, and duckweed."

My voice trailed off.

Glenn grunted. It wasn't clear whether he believed me or not.

Walking back to the car, Glenn spotted a horned lizard

Sandhill cranes fly over the marshes of Monte Vista Wildlife Refuge at sunrise

crouched motionless in the shade of a greasewood. Its hockey-puck-shaped body, no longer than my thumb, was covered with grayish-tan scales, almost exactly the color of the soil. It was a short-horned lizard, the only kind known from this arid, high-elevation environment. As we watched, it scuttled away across sunbaked ground where the only signs of water were long gone.

The sun began to sink over the San Juan Mountains as we turned south on Highway 285, circling around to the Monte Vista National Wildlife Refuge where we had begun the first day of spring. We cruised the road on the west edge of the refuge, looking for sandhill cranes in the marshes. The water was quiet, its surface reflecting only the changing light of evening. Finally we spotted the wide-winged birds in the air over the southwestern corner of the refuge. A small parade of cars led us to a flock of several hundred cranes feeding in the stubble of a cornfield. We were looking for a roost, a flock settling in for the night. But these birds were restless, leaping into the air and flying off in trailing lines, headed toward the other side of the valley miles away where a spiraling flock of cranes circled, climbing higher and higher into the sky. We couldn't tell where this distant gyre of cranes was headed, but we guessed that the unusually hot spring weather had them testing the wind, preparing for their journey north.

We spotted a swirl of sandhills landing in a dry field just outside the refuge boundary, drove over, and opened the windows. Their throbbing "khrrrrr, khrrrrr!" calls drew more cranes, flying over in groups, circling, and then dropping down to land, long legs outstretched. Soon there were hundreds of cranes feeding, calling, and leaping in a constantly moving mass of long-necked, gray-feathered bodies.

As the sun sank toward the horizon, Glenn grew restless too. He needed to get closer for good photos. Richard turned down a ditch road that led along one edge of the field; the van crept along until we were almost upon the flock. Glenn began shooting. The intensity of the cranes' calls increased. The birds, usually oblivious to car traffic, began to lift off by the tens and fifties, rising on wide wings into the sky, circling higher and higher. Group after group of sandhills lifted off, headed north and disappeared into the evening sky, trailed by the sound of those throaty calls.

Watching the cranes circle high overhead, I wondered how I, a relative newcomer, fit into this rich and paradoxical expanse of desert. Unlike Cano and his towers that sprout from a tradition stretching back to the miraculous appearance of the Virgin Mary at the site of an Aztec shrine four centuries ago, my relationship to this place is new. Unlike sandhill cranes, whose species' story stretches back millions of years to the days when the San Luis Valley was geologically young, my species' involvement in North America began only after the glaciers retreated a mere 12,000 years ago. Unlike the sand grains that build and rebuild the dunes, their scratched contours and the electrons

Several flocks of sandhill cranes spiral over the San Luis Valley in early spring

that hold their internal crystalline framework a record of the larger story of the valley's waves of sand, my life's story reveals nothing about this landscape. In terms of these long, complex, and revealing relationships, I am a mere beginner.

Yet I am connected. My bond with this high desert originates at the same level where any of us are connected to place: with the atoms that make up our bodies. The molecules that form our cells are the same atoms that shape the Earth. Atoms perform the most fundamental dance of life: they cycle from organism to landscape and back again, whirling in and out of different forms and phases to the beat of breath and digestion and the rearrangement of matter and material. The being I call "me" is formed of the same dancing atoms as those of the San Luis Valley's peaks, salt crusts, dunes, and marshes. Like the valley, I am a creature of water, more than ninety percent by volume, two-thirds by weight. The fluids that run through my veins and hydrate my cells are part salt, part fresh, no different than the water that animates this sere landscape.

In comparison with other species, humans are not particularly impressive. We have no fins to propel us from stream to ocean and back again, no wings to power us thousands of feet into the air, no jaws strong enough to crack deer vertebrae in one bite, no idea of how to metamorphose from caterpillar to butterfly, much less to wait out inhospitable decades as seeds. We have big brains, but they can be as much curse as blessing, leading us to imagine ourselves superior to the rest of life. What we do best comes not from our heads but our hearts, from an ineffable impulse that resists logic and definitions and calculation:

love. Love is what connects us to the rest of the living world, the divine urging from within that guides our best steps in the dance of life. Perhaps what allows a newcomer like me to belong to the valley is the same gift that allows humanity to belong to this rare blue planet: an ability to love its miraculous as well as its mundane. This paradoxical desert of water and sand, a place that dances in the wind and echoes with the throaty calls of sandhill cranes, reminds me of what it is to love with a whole heart, to be at home, no matter who I am, where I was born, or how long I stay.

When the sound of the sandhill cranes died away, Richard started the van and we drove up the San Luis Valley, following the lines of flying birds, all of us bound in our own way for home.

about the author

Susan J. Tweit is a field ecologist who began her career studying wildfires, shrubland ecology, and grizzly bear habitat in the Yellowstone region. She is the author of eight nonfiction books on the wild around us in the American West, dozens of articles and essays for magazines from *Audubon* to *Wilderness,* radio commentaries available on the Pacifica Radio Network, and columns for Writers on the Range, an op-ed syndicate carried in more than 80 western newspapers. She lives in the high desert of south-central Colorado with her husband, Richard Cabe, and her Great Dane, Isis.

about the photographer

Glenn Oakley is a widely published photographer whose work has consistently explored the landscape and how people relate to and treat the environment they inhabit. He has shot photos for commercial clients including Patagonia, L. L. Bean, and Volkswagen as well as for feature articles in magazines such as *Smithsonian, Outside, Backpacker,* and *Sunset.* He has contributed to hundreds of books and was the primary photographer for *Snake: The Plain and Its People, Frommer's Bed & Breakfasts in the Rocky Mountains,* and *Frommer's Bed & Breakfasts in New England.*

Library of Congress Cataloging-in-Publication Data

Tweit, Susan J.
    The San Luis Valley : sand dunes and sandhill cranes / text by Susan J. Tweit;
photographs by Glenn Oakley.
        p. cm. — (Desert places)
    ISBN-13: 978-0-8165-2424-2 (pbk. : alk. paper)
    ISBN-10: 0-8165-2424-6 (pbk. : alk. paper)
        1. San Luis Valley (Colo. and N.M.)—Description and travel. 2. San
Luis Valley (Colo. and N.M.)—Pictorial works. 3. San Luis Valley (Colo.
and N.M.)—History, Local. 4. San Luis Valley (Colo. and N.M.)—History.
5. Natural history—San Luis Valley (Colo. and N.M.) 6. Great Sand Dunes
National Park (Colo.) 7. Sandhill crane—San Luis Valley (Colo. and N.M.)
1. Oakley, Glenn, 1955– 11. Title. 111. Series.
    F782.S2T87 2005
    917.88'3—dc22
                                                        2005005823